Tenement Stories

Sean Price

Raintree

Chicago, Illinois

Designed by Michelle Lisseter, Kim Miracle,
and Bigtop
Printed in China

11 10 09 08
10 9 8 7 6 5

**Library of Congress
Cataloging-in-Publication Data**
Price, Sean.
  Tenement stories : immigrant life, 1835-1935 /
Sean Price.
     p. cm. -- (American history through primary
sources)
  Includes bibliographical references and index.
  ISBN 1-4109-2412-2 (hardcover) -- ISBN 1-4109-
2423-8 (pbk.)
  ISBN 978-1-4109-2412-4 (hardcover) -- ISBN 978-1-
4109-2423-0 (pbk.)
  1. Immigrants--Housing--United States--History--
Juvenile literature. 2.
Immigrants--Housing--United States--History--
Sources--Juvenile literature.
  3. Tenement houses--United States--History--Juvenile
literature. 4.
Tenement houses--United States--History--Sources--
Juvenile literature. 5.
United States--Emigration and immigration--Social
aspects--Juvenile
literature. 6. United States--Emigration and
immigration--Social
aspects--Sources--Juvenile literature. I. Title. II. Series.
  HD7288.72.U5P75 2006
  305.9'0691209747109034--dc22
                                        2006006580

Acknowledgments
The author and publisher are grateful to the
following for permission to reproduce copyright
material: The Art Archive/Culver Pictures **pp. 5**, **22**,
23; Bettmann/Corbis **pp. 10**, **14**, **20–21**; Corbis
pp. 11, **19**; Getty Images **pp. 15**, **29**; Hulton-
Deutsch Collection/Corbis **p. 25**; Library of Congress
Prints and Photographs Division **p. 24**; Museum of
the City of New York, The J. Clarence Davies
Collection **p. 9**; NY Municipal Archives **pp. 7**, **26**;
Photography Collection, Miriam and Ira D. Wallach
Division of Art. Prints and Photographs, the New
York Public Library, Astor, Lenox and Tilden
Foundations **p. 17**; Picture Collection, The Branch
Libraries, The New York Public Library, Astor, Lenox
and Tilden Foundations **pp. 12–13**; Rudy Briel **p. 27**.

Cover photograph of a New York City tenement
interior reproduced with permission of
Bettmann/Corbis.

Photo research by Tracy Cummins.

Illustrations by Darren Lingard.

The publishers would like to thank Nancy Harris
and Joy Rogers for their assistance in the preparation
of this book.

Every effort has been made to contact copyright
holders of any material reproduced in this book. Any
omissions will be rectified in subsequent printings if
notice is given to the publishers.

Disclaimer
All the Internet addresses (URLs) given in this book
were valid at the time of going to press. However,
due to the dynamic nature of the Internet, some
addresses may have changed, or sites may have
changed or ceased to exist since publication. While
the author and publishers regret any inconvenience
this may cause readers, no responsibility for any such
changes can be accepted by either the author or the
publishers.

It is recommended that adults supervise children on
the Internet.

Contents

Some words are printed in bold, **like this**. You can find out what they mean on page 30. You can also look in the box at the bottom of the page where they first appear.

Life in a New Land

People often move from one country to another. They are known as **immigrants**. In the 1800s, many immigrants came to the United States. Most of them had one thing in common. They wanted to start a new life in a new land.

Most immigrants lived in big cities. Many lived in New York City. Immigrants usually had little money. But they still needed places to live. So, they lived in **tenements**. Tenements are small, narrow apartment buildings.

The number of ▶ immigrants in the United States increased in the late 1800s and early 1900s.

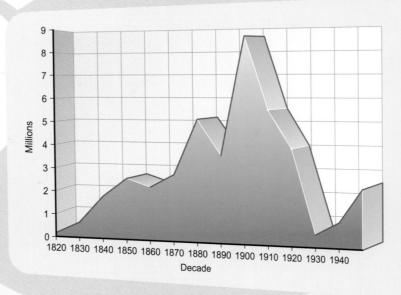

immigrant	person who moves from one country to another
tenement	small, narrow apartment building

Tenement life could be hard. The buildings might be crowded with too many people. But immigrant life could be exciting as well. The streets were always busy. There were many interesting people.

This book will show what life was like for immigrants living in tenements. Their experiences helped change life in the United States.

▼ Crowded streets were common in the tenement areas of New York.

5

Building the Tenements

The word **tenement** comes from "tenant-house." This means a house to rent.

Throughout the 1800s, **immigrants** came to New York City. They needed places to live. Big houses were divided into apartments. Soon, people built new apartment buildings instead. They called the newer buildings tenements as well.

In 1863 a new apartment building was built at 97 Orchard Street. It was owned by Lukas Glockner. He was an immigrant. The building was five stories tall. It was about as long as a pro basketball court. But it was only half as wide. The building had twenty apartments. Apartments were also called **flats**.

Families lived on the upper floors. There were businesses in the **basement**. A basement is a floor below ground. In time, there were businesses on the first floor, too. These businesses often sold hats and other items.

basement	floor of a building that is below ground
flat	apartment

▼ *This is the tenement at 97 Orchard Street.*

The Neighborhood

Orchard Street was in the Lower East Side of New York City (see map). The Lower East Side was crowded. **Immigrants** came here from many countries. They crowded into the **tenements**.

The neighborhood was noisy. Horses clip-clopped on the streets. Street sellers called out in different languages. There were strong odors everywhere. Some of these odors smelled really bad. They smelled like old fish or worse. Others smelled good. There were good smells of food cooking.

Teenagers often worked full time. Many carried big bundles of cloth to neighborhood clothes makers. Others went to school.

Street games

Children often played on the streets of the Lower East Side. Boys liked to play "One o' Cat." This was like baseball. The players hit a block of wood instead of a ball.

Girls played games like "Ring Around the Rosie." Children played this game by holding hands and walking in a circle. They sang "Ring Around the Rosie" as they walked.

▼ *This is a map of the Lower East Side.*

9

Tenement Life

Tenement life was usually crowded. Each **flat** (apartment) in a tenement building usually had three to four rooms. The front rooms got sunlight and air. The back rooms were sometimes dark and stuffy.

Immigrants usually had big families. Even so, they often took in **boarders**. Boarders were people who paid rent to live there, too. Most flats were built for one family. But to save money, two families often lived in one flat. Many people often had to sleep in one bedroom.

Most flats were ▶ very small. Many people shared the tiny rooms.

boarder	person who pays rent to live in a house
stoop	stairway leading from the street to a building's front door

▼ *People in tenements had no air conditioning or fans.*

Hokeypokey man

On summer evenings, kids looked for the "hokeypokey man." He sold ice cream for a penny.

People on the Lower East Side stayed outside a lot in warm weather. Adults talked on the **stoop**. A stoop is a stairway. It leads from the street to the front door.

Tenement fires could ▼
kill people or leave
them homeless.

Fire and heating

Fire was a constant worry for people living in **tenements**. Their apartment buildings were made mostly of brick on the outside. But inside, they were made of wood. This could burn easily.

People often used fire in **flats** (apartments). They burned candles for light. People also used lamps that burned kerosene (a fuel) or oil.

Cooking stoves burned **coal**. Coal is a rock that burns well. The stove was often the only source of heat. In winter, parents put children's beds near the stove. This helped keep them warm. But it was also dangerous.

In summer, tenements were too hot to stay inside. Some people slept on the roof or the **fire escape**. The fire escape was a small metal balcony outside a window. It had a ladder leading down to the street. This allowed people to escape during a fire.

coal	black or brown rock that burns easily
fire escape	metal stairway that allows people to escape from a building during a fire

Washing

Monday was laundry day for **immigrants** living on the Lower East Side. Back then, water was not piped into buildings. People got their water from a hand pump downstairs.

People did the laundry down near the pump. Young children played together in the **alley**. An alley is a narrow area between two buildings.

People dried their ▼
laundry on wash
lines stretched
across the alley.

14

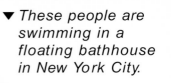

▼ These people are swimming in a floating bathhouse in New York City.

When it was cold, people did their washing inside. Then, they had to carry big, heavy pans of water up the stairs.

During the summer months, people could get clean in floating bathhouses. These were like big swimming areas.

alley   narrow area between two buildings

Staying healthy

Early **tenement** buildings did not have indoor bathrooms. People used **privies** (outhouses). These were bathrooms that were outside. At night, people might use a bowl called a **chamber pot** instead. They emptied the chamber pot into the privy each morning.

In the 1800s, people did not know that washing their hands was important. This led to many terrible illnesses. One illness was **cholera**. It is a disease spread by unwashed hands. Cholera is also spread by dirty water. In 1866 and 1892, the Lower East Side was hit by cholera **epidemics**. Epidemics are when many people get a disease.

By early 1905, all tenements had to have sinks and running water. This helped people stay clean.

This child is bathing and ▶ cleaning her clothes at the same time.

chamber pot	bowl used for going to the bathroom
cholera	disease spread by unwashed hands and dirty water
epidemic	widespread outbreak of disease
privy	outhouse

Work and Play

Immigrants held many different jobs. A lot of people who lived on the Lower East Side made clothes. Six out of ten people did this type of work. Some immigrants were very skilled at sewing and needlepoint.

Each morning, workers went to **factories**. Factories are buildings where products are made. People worked ten to twelve hours a day. They used fast-moving machinery. This made the work dangerous. Factory workers only made about $1.25 per day.

Many people in **tenements** turned their homes into small factories. Some people called these places **sweatshops**. Workers in sweatshops made little money. They worked long hours.

Rent costs

In the late 1800s, rent was around eight to ten dollars a month.

factory   building where products are made
sweatshop   factory that pays little for working long hours

Whole families might work making clothes or rolling cigars. They also hired outside help. The workers were paid for each item they made. Sometimes families had to work through the night to pay the monthly rent.

Many people worked in ▼ apartment sweatshops like this one.

Going to school

Many **immigrant** children had to work. Their families needed this extra money to survive. Often their parents never went to school themselves.

Other immigrants expected their children to go to school. They wanted a better life for their children. Most immigrant children went to **public schools**. These schools were paid for by the city.

Lower East Side schools were overcrowded. In 1906 a newspaper called *Forward* reported about one neighborhood school. It said, "In the Henry Street school there are eighty children in a classroom built for forty."

Candy store clubs

Many immigrant children learned skills at club meetings. These clubs met at local candy stores. Clubs might teach music. They might teach children how to play cards or sports.

20

Children often worked during the day. Then they went to school at night. It was hard for them to stay awake in class. Even so, many children learned and did well.

▼ Schools on the Lower East Side were crowded.

21

The Lower East Side ▲ had few parks. Kids played in **alleys**. They also played on the sidewalks and streets.

Fun and games

Baseball was a popular sport among **immigrants**. People used almost anything they could find as bases. "We used to play in the street whenever the policeman wasn't around," one man told the *New York Tribune* in 1900. This is a newspaper. The man grew up on the Lower East Side.

Tenement kids knew many games. Shooting marbles was popular. Boys played "Prisoner." Teams took turns capturing players. Many games could be played in the hallway. They could also be played on the rooftop.

Girls were not allowed to play rough like boys. They enjoyed hopscotch and jumping rope.

Families from the Lower East Side liked to go to Coney Island. Coney Island was an amusement park. It was in nearby Long Island. Families could go on rides. They could swim at the beach. They could also pay to see animals such as elephants and lions.

Going to Coney Island ▼
was a fun trip for many immigrants.

Improving the Tenements

Jacob Riis was an **immigrant**. He worked as a newspaper reporter. His job took him to the Lower East Side a lot. Riis was upset by the terrible living conditions he saw there. In 1890 he wrote a book called *How the Other Half Lives*. It was about the rough conditions in the **tenements**.

Riis photographed the things he saw. Drawings based on his photos appeared in his book. These images shocked the public. People demanded cleaner and healthier immigrant neighborhoods.

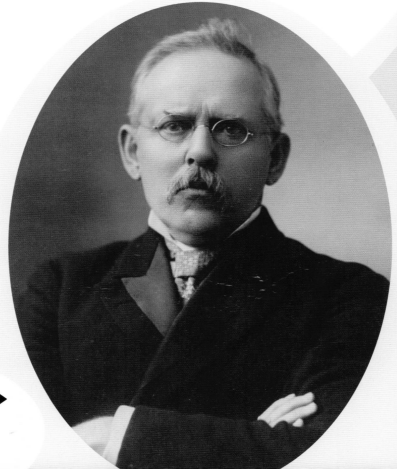

Jacob Riis worked ▶ *hard to improve tenement life.*

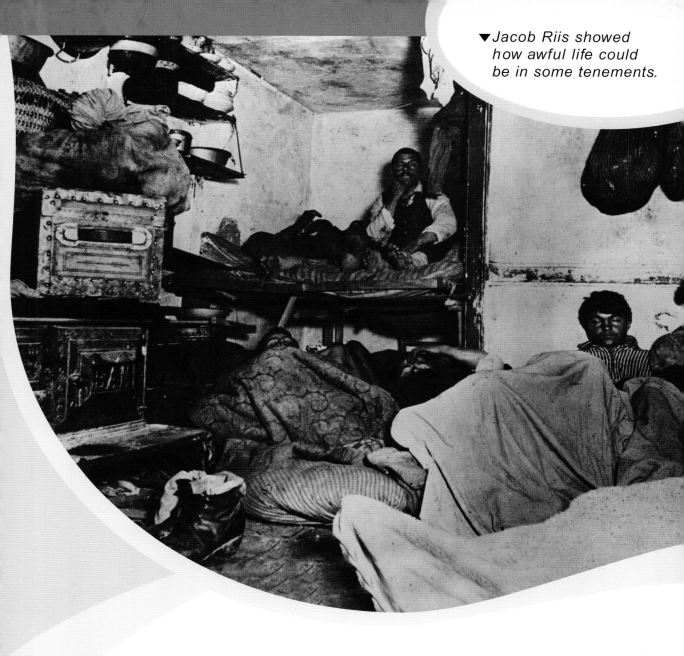

In time, owners had to fix run-down buildings. They were forced to put lights in hallways. They also had to add toilets and sinks inside. The city began to build neighborhood parks. Children could finally play somewhere other than the streets.

From tenement to museum

The improvements did not help much. By the 1930s, more than half the **tenements** still did not have good heating. One in six tenements still did not have hot water.

Between 1934 and 1935, the State of New York forced owners to fix up the tenements. Some tenement owners did improve the buildings. **Flats** (apartments) finally had good heating and hot water.

▼ This is a tenement kitchen from 1935. It is much nicer than older tenement kitchens.

▼ Today, 97 Orchard Street is a museum. It shows what tenement life was like.

But many tenement owners could not make these changes. They did not have enough money. By 1935, 97 Orchard Street and many other tenements closed.

Luckily, 97 Orchard Street was not torn down. Its flats remained empty until 1988. That year, the building became the Tenement Museum. It is now one of New York's most popular historic sites.

A Song from the Lower East Side

Songwriter Irving Berlin (1888–1989) was an **immigrant**. He became famous for writing hit tunes. "White Christmas" and "God Bless America" are two of his most famous songs.

Berlin was born with the name Israel Baline. Many people in show business changed their names in the early 1900s. Israel changed his name too.

Berlin was the youngest of eight children. He grew up in the Lower East Side. He left home at a young age. He had little schooling. At first, Berlin earned money by singing on the streets. Soon, he sang at restaurants as well. People liked Berlin's singing. He began to write his own songs.

Berlin's first hit song came in 1911. It was "Alexander's Ragtime Band." He went on to write songs for many musical plays. One popular musical was *Annie Get Your Gun*. Berlin also wrote songs about life in the Lower East Side.

Many of Irving ▶ Berlin's songs are still popular today.

Glossary

alley narrow area between two buildings

basement floor of a building that is below ground

boarder person who pays rent to live in a house

chamber pot bowl used for going to the bathroom

cholera disease spread by unwashed hands and dirty water

coal black or brown rock that burns easily

epidemic widespread outbreak of disease

factory building where products are made

fire escape metal stairway that allows people to escape from a building during a fire

flat apartment

immigrant person who moves from one country to another

privy outhouse

public school school paid for by the government

stoop stairway leading from the street to a building's front door

sweatshop factory that pays little for working long hours

tenement small, narrow apartment building

Want to Know More?

Books to read

- Granfield, Linda, and Arlene Alda (photographer). *97 Orchard Street, New York: Stories of Immigrant Life.* Toronto: Tundra, 2001.

- Hopkinson, Deborah. *Shutting out the Sky: Life in the Tenements of New York, 1880–1924.* New York: Orchard, 2003.

Websites

- http://www.tenement.org Explore tenement life for yourself by visiting the Lower East Side Tenement Museum's website.

- http://americanhistory.si.edu/sweatshops/index.htm "Between a Rock and a Hard Place: A History of American Sweatshops, 1820–Present" is an exhibition at the Smithsonian's National Museum of American History. Learn all about it at this site.

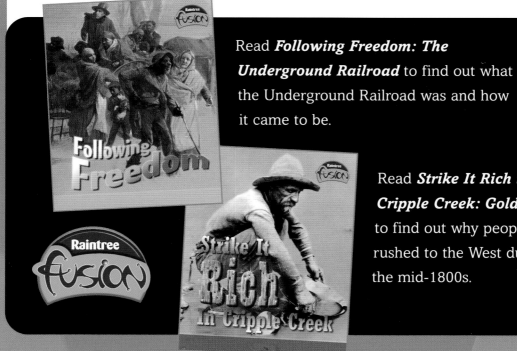

Read *Following Freedom: The Underground Railroad* to find out what the Underground Railroad was and how it came to be.

Read *Strike It Rich in Cripple Creek: Gold Rush* to find out why people rushed to the West during the mid-1800s.

Index